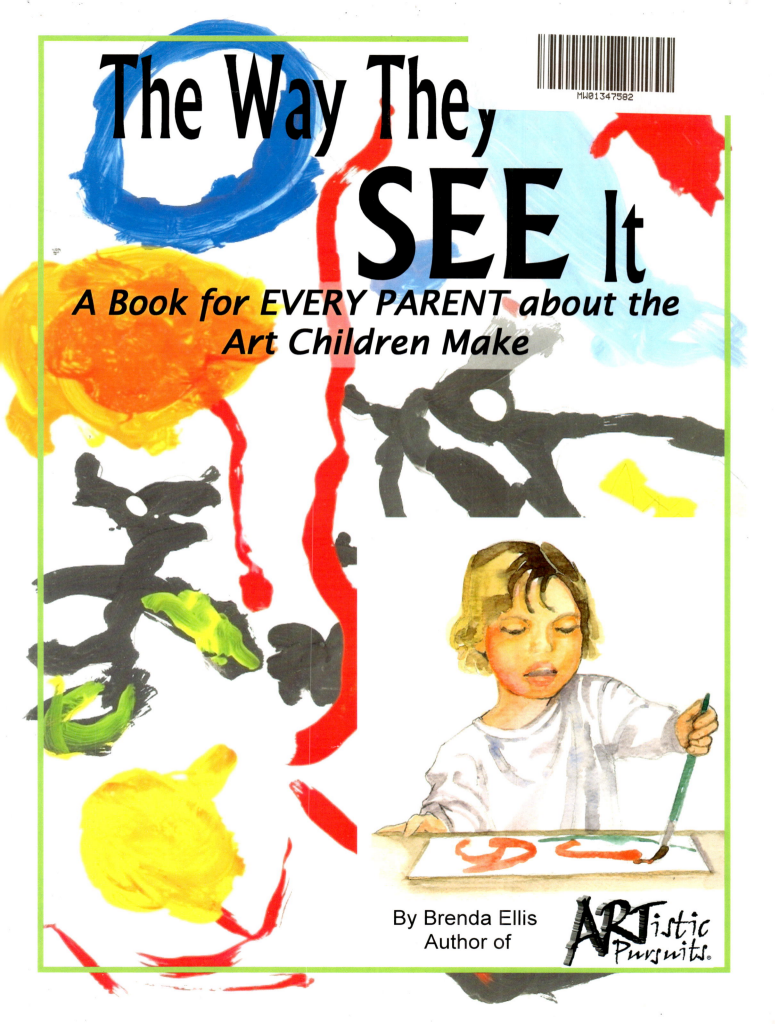
The Way They SEE It

A Book for EVERY PARENT about the Art Children Make

By Brenda Ellis
Author of ARTistic Pursuits

The Way They SEE It

A Book for EVERY PARENT about the Art Children Make

Written by Brenda Ellis
Author of *ARTistic Pursuits®* art program for grades K-12
Edited by Ariel DeWitt
Illustrations and photographs by Brenda Ellis
Children's artworks were created by children Brenda has worked with in public and private settings from 1985-2008. Art works by the masters provided by Dover Publications Inc., NY.

Second Edition

Copyright © 2007, 2008, 2011 by Brenda Ellis
All rights reserved. No portion of this book may be reproduced – mechanically, electronically, or by any other means, including photocopying. This book is only produced in full color. If you have a black and white copy, it has been produced illegally. Please don't compromise the educational value of this book by photocopying images. Children cannot see what a pencil drawing or color work should look like when color and tonal values are reduced to black and white.

Printed in the U.S.A.
ISBN 978-0-9815982-0-8

Published by
Artistic Pursuits Inc.
Northglenn, Colorado
www.artisticpursuits.com
alltheanswers@artisticpursuits.com

A Different Kind of Book

This book is for Mommy, Daddy, and any adult who desires to give a child of three, four, or five an early experience with the process of making art. It is not a coloring book. It is not an activity book. It begins at the true beginning of any artistic production, seeing. We can only make art from what we know. If we want our children to create original works of art, then they must be made aware of the world in which they live. Caring adults can nurture this awareness and bring it to life in a child. This book shows you how. Discussions on the nature of children's artistic development will help you see and understand your child's art better. You will learn methods of teaching by using real world examples that work with the purposes children have for making art. Creating art has more going for it than making pretty pictures. Making art requires children to make their own decisions about their picture and that produces sharper thinking skills. Communication skills develop as children talk about the pictures they produce. This book will suggest ways to turn art times into real educational experiences, resulting in enthusiastic artists who are ready to learn more, see more, and create more art. You will want to check out the FIRST SKILLS section on page 71 if your child is using art tools and materials for the first time. While the projects in this section seem very simple, they are important first steps in gaining the skills necessary to produce art of any kind. No previous knowledge of art concepts is required on the part of the adult or child. No rigid schedule is necessary. Use the projects whenever you are looking for an activity that will engage and awaken your little one's senses.

DEDICATION

This book is dedicated to my dad and mom, Clifford and Juanita, who enjoyed the beauty of the world and encouraged me to take a look. I remember Dad's fascination with Kansas sunsets, rains storms, and baby animals. I especially thank Mom for allowing me to watch as she practiced art and for letting me know that artistic skill was valued by supplying me with art materials during my entire childhood.

Contents

Page	Lesson		
4	Materials		

Section One – The Nature of Children's Artistic Development

Page		Lesson	
5			
7	1	It's About the Process	
9			Discover Art Project
10	2	Learning from Parents and on Their Own	
12			The Sky I See Project
13	3	Those Lovely Scribbles	
15			Mark-Making Project
16	4	Playing with Materials	
18			Dough Project
19	5	Curiosity	
21			Impressions Project
22	6	Adding More to the Picture	
24			Favorite Things Project
25	7	Inventing a Story	
27			Telling a Story Project
28	8	Beyond Seeing	
30			Me Project
31	9	Inventing a Language of Symbols	
34			Direct Observation Project
35	10	Opportunity	
37			Puppet Project

Section Two – Use Real World Examples to Point out Artistic Ideas

Page		Lesson	
38			
41	11	Creativity	
43			My Hand Project
44	12	Invite the Story	
46			What I Did Project
47	13	Visual Awareness	
49			Plant Project
50	14	Absorbing Pictures	
53			Story Book Picture Project
54	15	Art to Retell an Event	
56			Trip Project
57	16	The Study	
59			Visual Note Taking Project
60	17	Encouragement	
62			How Big I Am Project
63	18	Seeing the World Through a Child's Eyes	
66			Horizon Line Project
67	19	Where Do They Go from Here?	
70			The Way I SEE It Project

Section Three – First Skills   Scissors, Pencil, Crayon, and Marker, Adhesives, Brushes and Paint

Page	Lesson
71	
87	Bibliography

Materials
Good Preschool Art Supplies

Crayons:

Crayola® is the only brand I suggest in crayons. Other crayon brands are too waxy and have little pigment. Since getting color on the paper is what it is all about, it makes sense to use crayons like Crayola®. Purchase sets of 64 or more so children have a wide variety of color choices. Children under three may need Large Size Crayola® Sets, which will not break as easily in their hands. Crayola® also makes glitter, metallic, scented, washable, and triangular crayons.

Markers:

Our favorite is **Mr. Sketch® Scented Markers by Sanford.** Broad tips are easy for preschoolers to handle and they smell like strawberries, grapes and yummy things. Other marker brands, found in the children's art section, will do just as well. Mr. Sketch® also makes unscented and washable markers.

Paint:

Not all paints are equal in quality. **Prang®** and **Crayola®** are good brands. **Rose Art®, Reeves®, Sargent®,** and others brands found on department store shelves have less pigment, resulting in less color brightness. Any paint labeled "washable" will have much less pigment and color brightness. Tempera paints will seem too gel-like, resulting in poor coverage. Preschoolers may not notice these differences so it is more important to choose a paint *type* that is easiest to handle. Children three and under prefer liquid paints, while 4 and 5 year olds can move on to dry pigments, where water must be added. Use cheap soft brushes until the child is drawing in fine lines and needs greater detail. Then choose a brush that comes to a point and holds its shape.

Finger Paint:

Finger paints can be purchased or made from household ingredients such as liquid starch or wheat paste. See the home-made mixture on page fifteen.

Clay:

Use **Play-Doh®** or the home-made dough mixture on page eighteen, which is easily manipulated and reusable. Neither is meant to be preserved and will crack if left out in the open to dry. **Play Doh®** is found in toy departments rather than art departments because it is made by Hasbro. Clays, both natural and polymer, are too stiff for small hands.

Paper:

Purchase a ream of **copy paper**, any brand, from the local office supply store. Use copy paper for coloring, drawing, and painting. Children who work on a painting so long that the paper tears do need a sturdier paper, but most of the time you can avoid buying expensive pads of art paper. Rolls of paper are fun and useful for preschoolers. Construction paper adds color to projects and is good for cutting and gluing, but not for painting.

Section One

The Nature of Children's Artistic Development

Children's art is often a puzzle to adults. By understanding why children make art and the nature of how it develops, we can gain a perspective that allows us to appreciate what they produce at any age. We will also gain confidence that skills are being developed even though a child's approach may be highly unusual or individual.

Family Portrait by Ariel, age 2 ½. From left to right, brother, me, Mommy (pregnant), and Daddy.

Let's consider what children's art looks like. Those who work with children will soon notice that children's artistic talents progress through specific stages. The stages of development are as natural as progressing from a crawl to a walk, and when they are older, on to a 100 yard dash. We can think about the three, four, and five-year-old as being in the crawl to walk stage of artistic skills. In art, these skills first involve using the large muscle groups (arms) and gain skill using small muscle groups (fingers).

The paintings below show the two stages of development that a preschool child will work within: manipulation and symbolic. On the left is an example of manipulation of materials. The paint is put onto the paper just to see what it will do, with no concern for showing an object. Next to it is a representation of a snake. The child works at creating her own symbols that stand for the objects she wishes to put on paper. Preschoolers will bounce back and forth between these two modes of making art as they learn about the materials themselves and develop a symbolic language.

Grown-up Talk
It's about the Process

What a delight when our little ones initiate a creative project. I remember when my first child flipped an ice cube tray upside down and inserted his crayons into the slots to make a birthday cake for his stuffed animals. I was delighted at his inventiveness. I've pondered the creative aspect of children ever since.

Recently my niece told me of an experience with her three-year-old son, Tanner. He got the creative urge and wanted to make something out of a paper tube. So they set out to make something with pipe cleaners, tissue paper, and other materials. The object they created had wings, antenna, and was quite colorful as she describes it. They had two hours of fun. I could tell she felt the satisfaction of giving him her time and attention. Her son's delight with the results was obvious when he wanted to take it to Grandma's house to show her. Imagine my niece's disappointment to find that Tanner had striped the prized artistic work down to the bare tube by the time they arrived. But upon arrival, he asked Grandma for some paint. He spent another two hours painting the tube repeatedly, and again he was quite pleased with the results.

In my niece's mind, her time had been wasted. It is quite common for adults to think that the purpose for a creative project is about the finished product or the result. We all understand how important this little treasure was to Mom because it was a creation of her son's and a symbol of their time spent together. Adults must find the courage to set aside such sentimentality for the greater purpose of understanding the needs of our children. Tanner had stumbled onto something quite exciting during his two hours with Mom that day. He learned to take a simple form and add to it in whatever ways his mind could come up with. His imagination drew from the wealth of stories read to him, visual experiences, and everything he knew about his world in order to make something entirely new that was truly his own creation. What an experience his Mom had given him! Who knows what creative thoughts entered his mind as he rode to Grandma's house that day? What else could it do? What could it become with paint?

Children become quite focused when creating. For the child, it's about the PROCESS not the RESULTS. This is old news in children's art education, but not many art teachers or parents grasp the importance of allowing children to experiment and enjoy the process of working with the materials. I hope you begin to ponder the idea now. Watch your children. Think about what they may be learning through the process of what they are doing when they create. You can watch their little faces and see that their minds are fully engaged, thinking, pondering, creating! You don't have to identify the benefits or explain the results of their time to anyone else. Just know that by allowing them to create you are giving them time to practice something good that they will be able to draw from for a lifetime.

Children learn through the process of using the materials. First efforts with any type of material will be experimental and unlike the adult who may be focused on the end result, the child will be fully engaged in the process all along the way.

Picture Talk

Ambrosius Bosschaert, *Bouquet of Flowers on a Ledge*, c. 1620.
Photo Credit: Dover Publications Inc.

The artist made a picture of bright and colorful flowers. Find a flower that is yellow. Find a flower that is red. There are more than flowers in this picture. On the tabletop is a black shell with white speckles. Can you find it? Can you find a yellow shell with white inside? A little bug crawls out of one of the flowers. Where is it? Can you find a butterfly and a dragonfly?

Discover Art Project

With your child, explore the connection between real objects and objects in pictures. Gather objects similar to those in the painting of *Bouquet of Flowers on a Ledge* by Ambrosius Bosschaert. Shells, flowers, leaves, and bugs might be found. Allow your child to touch and explore the objects. Name the objects and name the colors. Use any descriptive words that you think of. Provide crayons and paper. When working with children who have not made art in the past, model making art by drawing beside them, each using your own paper and making your own pictures. Do not draw on the child's picture, but allow it to be her own.

You just explored some interesting objects. Artists draw and paint those things on paper. Making a picture is a way of keeping special things near us. Draw a picture of some of the things you explored or things you saw in the painting of a bouquet of flowers. Use your crayons on paper.

Hold a crayon like this.

The crayon is held in place by the thumb and two fingers. Pointer finger holds the top and the middle finger holds the side opposite the thumb. See page seventy-seven for further instructions.

This art was made by a young artist. Do you like the colors?

Your child just looked at a work of art and discovered objects that are both beautiful and interesting. By looking at pictures, especially art, your child will find reasons to make his own. He will pick up new information from pictures, make connections to things he already knows and sees in his own world, and he will become familiar with seeing a three-dimensional world on a flat surface. Children love pictures of all kinds. During their first year, they are able to connect real world objects to pictures of those objects and name them. Fine art, photographs, and illustrations offer a wide variety of visual information. A great book to look at is *A Child's Book of Art, Great Pictures First Words* by Lucy Micklethwait.

Grown-up Talk
Learning from Parents and on Their Own

The BEST place for your child to learn is right beside you. A parent's interests, talents, and abilities are meant to be shared with their children. Don't worry about what you don't know. Children love learning right alongside their parents, as they pick up new skills. Parents teach children how to learn when they challenge themselves to learn new things and then meet those challenges with laughter and fun. Children learn from adults by observing, listening to, and mimicking what adults see, say, and show. Be aware of your own perfectionism, expectations that are beyond the experience level of the child, and a too narrow focus on the end product. These negative qualities are ones that children quickly pick up when parents display them. Once children take hold of these ideas, they get discouraged and want to quit making art. Parents can model making art with a playful, light-hearted attitude and enjoyment in the process involved.

Children also learn on their own, through exploration and experimentation. We can teach them to be better learners by purposefully engaging them in activities that use both of these natural ways of learning. They will observe with you, then you will set your children free to explore (learn) by using their own hands and ideas. When working with 3, 4 and 5 year-olds, keep in mind that the process of creation is more important to them than the results. It is also more important to their development. Do not cut for them, but teach them how to hold scissors correctly. Do not draw for them, but point out the curve of a leaf using your fingers to trace its edges. By allowing children to handle new materials and new information, they learn the techniques common to art. They acquire skills that they will not acquire if an adult handles everything for them in order to make it look good. Most importantly, when a project is completed by the child, he will feel a sense of accomplishment in the end that will generate confidence.

> Children learn best and remember more when learning is connected to an emotion such as joy or excitement. Close contact with an adult that holds, hugs, talks about, and gets excited about things seen in the world helps a child to remember his experiences in more detail. A baseball game viewed from Dad's lap will make a more lasting impression than a game viewed while among a group of classmates, where the child experiences no personal interaction related to the game.

Picture Talk

El Greco, *View of Toledo*, c. 1604-14. Photo Credit: Dover Publications Inc.

This is a painting of Toledo, a city in the country of Spain. It was painted 400 years ago by a man called El Greco, which means "The Greek". In this picture, we see dark clouds of a storm. The clouds block the sunlight. . What words can you use to tell me what this sky looks like? Are the clouds **big**? Are the clouds **dark**? Are some parts of the sky **blue**? Are some parts bright **white**? Does the storm look **scary**?

The Sky I See Project

LOOK UP! We might call the sky blue, but look again. You can see many colors in the sky. Do you see blues that are different? Do you see other colors? Many things happen in the sky that changes the colors you see. During a sunset, you might see orange, pinks, or purples in the sky. There are many colors in our world and they keep changing so it is always interesting to look at.

Take your crayon box outdoors and look at the sky. Look in different directions. Find colors in your box that look like the colors in the sky. Then color a picture of the sky you see.

Hold a crayon like this.

The crayon is held in place by the thumb and two fingers. Pointer finger holds the top and the middle finger holds the side opposite the thumb. See page seventy-seven for further instructions.

Below are some skies that other children saw.

Grown-up Talk
Those Lovely Scribbles

With the multitudes of "washable" art products available on the shelves of our local department stores, we can safely assume that mark-making (in places we adults don't want it) is a common problem. The truth about this activity is that it is a necessary part of each child's artistic development. Let's look at the very real temptation that mark-making presents. Children are entranced by lines and squiggles, those magical marks that flow directly from their arm and are so clearly controlled by them. The joy of making a motion and leaving its mark behind to see is exhilarating! It is so inspiring that it takes no time at all to fill up an entire wall or ones entire body with wonderful marks. Mark-making, more commonly referred to as scribbling, is a natural phase of a child's development in the arts. One must first see what the materials can do before one goes on to representational drawing. The young child is not only seeing what the material can do, but is using large and small muscle groups to see what his arm and fingers can do. That's a lot of experimental learning. When adult responses are negative toward this activity, the child could shut down a very natural response that is designed to develop eye-hand coordination. Think of mark-making as an activity that has little to do with making a recognizable finished product. Allow mark-making. Just as we do not stop a baby from crawling, we should not stop a child from mark-making, recognizing it as an important first step.

Children can and should learn that making marks is a specific type of activity that they do in a specific place with specific tools. Just as Mommy cooks on the kitchen counter, and mixes messy things using a bowl, art is made at the kitchen table (or wherever) with art materials using a piece of paper. Sit down with your child, get out pencils and paper and make marks. See what the pencil can do. Put away art materials and bring them out again at another time. Children who learn to care for their art supplies, by using them in the way the parent has demonstrated in times together, can be trusted with more freedom. Freedom to use art supplies whenever the child chooses should be gained, and it can be earned by responsible behavior.

Picture Talk

Stanton MacDonald-Wright, *Abstraction on Spectrum (Organization, 5)*. C. 1914-17. Photo Credit: Dover Publications Inc., NY

This artist made marks with beautiful colors. Can you find a circle that is light blue? Can you find a circle that is orange? Can you find a triangle that is green? Can you find a triangle that is purple?

Mark-making Project

You can do so many things with your hands. You can scoop up a handful of sand. You can hold a spoon and maybe even push a button through a button hole. You can make art with your hands too. These children are making marks on paper with their hands and fingers. You can use one finger at a time, all of your fingers at once, or the side of your hand to make marks.

Tape a large sheet of paper (about 18"x18") onto a newspaper covered table surface. Pour ½ cup of finger paint onto the paper. Allow a child to play on the paper to get a feel for what can be done. This is a very tactile experience and most children love it, although some do not like to get their hands messy. Children may choose not to make a representational drawing. It is good if they choose to simply play or manipulate the paint. This project is great for experimental play because the marks can be wiped out again and again for a fresh start. You can use more than one color on any single work as well.

Student works are shown below.

Finger Paint Recipes:

1. Boil liquid starch until thick, and then add tempera or food coloring.
Or 2. Mix wheat paste (wallpaper paste) and water, and then add tempera or food color.

The paint should be thick like pudding. Some people use pudding! Use slick paper like Reynold's Freezer Paper or Butcher paper for best results.

Grown-up Talk
Playing with Materials

Part of the fun in art is in experimenting with the properties of the materials. Children love to explore the possibilities. They find that crayons are hard and make colorful marks. They can press hard to make a darker mark or lightly to make light marks. They have many color choices. Paint offers fewer color choices, but when colors run into each other all kinds of surprises happen on the paper. Applying color with a brush is exciting too. Dough is entirely different. It requires squeezing, pushing, and rolling the material. These are a child's experiences. As they work, children are learning all kinds of things about the material and what it can and can't do. Children may be so interested in working with the material that they do not make a "thing". It is easy to look at the results and think that their time or the materials have been wasted. However, when a child is actually engaged in experimenting with the material, lots of learning is taking place. This child may make a "thing" the next time or the time after that. I do not push children into making a "final something" when they seem to be enjoying the process of working with the material.

Art supplies can be manageable. Keep non-messy art supplies within easy reach of the child once the child has demonstrated that he can care for them and put them away. This could include only pencils and paper or may include crayons and markers as well. Art supplies should never be thrown in with toys. If uncared for in this way, crayons will break and markers and dough will dry out and become unusable. Messy art supplies, such as paint, should be managed and brought out when the parent chooses to allow the child to have an experience with them. In this way, parents control where and how the paints will be used. Messes can be monitored. Hard floors are excellent places to make paintings. Children do not tire of working on the floor and spills are cleaned up easily, especially on vinyl or tile floors. The floor could be covered with a canvas drop cloth or newspapers, although newspapers are made with an ink that will rub off on skin (a new development of the last 20 years). To keep brushes in good condition parents must give a final rinse to all brushes, even though children have rinsed them in a rinse can. Once a child has finished painting, the paints can be put away out of reach.

Picture Talk

Ammi Phillips, *Girl in Red with Her Cat and Dog*. c. 1834-36. Photo Credit: Dover Publications Inc., NY.

A girl posed for this painting with her cat and dog. Do you have pets? What kind of pets do you have? Pets often appear in works of art. Consider using your pet in your next work of art.

Dough Project

Dough feels good. What can you do with the dough? Can you **pound** it? Can you **squeeze** it? Can you **poke** it? Can you **pinch** it? Can you **roll** it? What happens if you roll it **back and forth**? What happens if you roll it **in all directions**?

I like to suggest words that give children ideas for how to handle the dough. Allow children to play using just their hands. On another day, give them tools from your kitchen to experiment with. Children will model the kinds of things that they draw. A snake is a favorite subject because once the clay is rolled back and forth; the result is recognized by most children as a snake. This kind of discovery is wonderful. Do not feel that you need to suggest these types of ideas. Some children who have difficulty drawing will find that they are very proficient at modeling a three-dimensional object. Others who feel comfortable drawing may have difficulty forming an object from dough. They may want to flatten it like paper and draw into it. That is OK, but eventually you will want to encourage that child to make a form that "stands up". Usually they will discover this on their own when you allow lots of undirected playtime. By allowing time to experiment, you will be helping the child to gain more experience and soon the one who found it difficult will have no difficulties at all.

Why Dough, Not Clay?

Dough is typically softer and easier to manipulate than clay. Dough is made from plant products while clays are dirt from the earth or polymers (plastic based.) I highly suggest **Play-Doh®** by Hasbro for small hands, but you don't have to buy it. Try the recipe below.

Ingredients	Instructions
2 cups water ½-cup salt Food coloring 2 tablespoons oil 2 tablespoons alum (Find this in spices) 2 cups white flour A pan A heavy spoon	1. Boil water, salt, and food coloring in the pan. 2. Remove pan from heat. Mix in oil, alum, and flour. 3. Return to medium heat and stir continuously until the liquid mixture forms a stiff ball, with no gooey mixture left. 4. Remove from pan. Let it cool slightly. While warm, knead for 5 minutes. 5. Clay can be used when cool. Store in a plastic container or bag to be used again.

Cooking oil makes the dough easier to work with and less sticky. Alum keeps the dough from molding so that it can be reused.

Grown-up Talk
Curiosity

Learning is motivated by curiosity. For the young, much of it is physical. While waiting for my daughter one day, I witnessed a very young child toddling after his mother down a sidewalk. Suddenly he stopped. He was face to face with a lion's head. Part of the ornamentation of the building, this six inch head stood only two feet from the ground and was out of view of most people who passed by. He immediately began interacting with it by inserting his tiny hand into the mouth and placing his fingers into its nostrils. Petting its mane and touching the protruding eyes and beard, he repeated all of these same actions again and again. Mom watched from about six feet away for quite some time, then walked over to him and squatted down. The young boy began verbalizing his excitement about this creature. His extremely limited vocabulary did not limit his excitement or his desire to share everything about the fascinating creature with his mother. She listened, nodded, smiled. She finally encouraged him to walk away and following her. He walked eight feet only to run into a second lion head. He immediately began exploring it as intensely as he had the first head and again Mom waited and watched. This young mother may have recognized the educational value of this experience for her child or perhaps she was just fascinated at watching her darling little boy be so excited, as I was. Whatever her reasons for patiently waiting, what she gave her son that day was an extremely valuable educational experience. This experience was motivated by his curiosity. He spent fifteen minutes interacting with a highly interesting three-dimensional object in which he measured size, by inserting hands and fingers. He explored form by touching the snout and mane. Proportions were examined by exploring facial features of a slightly different nature than those of his mother's face. Rushed children will not have time to gain this knowledge. The hectic lifestyle that most adults take upon themselves does not encourage children to explore their curiosity and learn from it. Real world experiences and the ability to process and share those experiences with a listening adult is where real learning takes place.

Make a conscious effort to enter into your child's learning pace. Give your children time to explore and to gather knowledge about the world he inhabits.

Picture Talk

Oscar E. Berninghaus (1874-1952) Peace *and Plenty*, 1925. Photo Credit: Dover Publications Inc.

The woman in this picture holds an ear of corn. Ornamental corn has hard kernels of many colors. Have you ever seen and touched ornamental corn? Do the kernels feel rough? How do you think the husks on the corn feel?
How do you think the pumpkins feel? The way something feels is called its texture. How would you describe the texture of the feather head dress that hangs on the wall in this painting?

Impressions Project

Make your own impressions in Play-Doh®. Explore items around your house or outside that have interesting textures. You may find a rough shell or a rough piece of wood. Each object makes a different impression. Gather as many objects as you can find.

Make a ball of dough. Place it on the table and then roll over it with a rolling pin or wooden dowel until it has a smooth surface. Make several of these at a time. Next, take a textured object and press it into the clay. Lift and see what kind of impression the object made. You can explore with as many objects as you like.

Pine cone

Pine cone impression

Pine needles

Pine needles impression

Grown-up Talk
Adding More to the Picture

Young children do not approach the picture as a whole space, using foreground, background, or negative space (the area around the objects), so the work will not look like the work of an adult artist. To help the child meet his goals we must let go of the adult goal of making a "pretty, well composed picture". Children are focused on the "things" in their picture. The marks they make stand for the things that are important in telling the story. Once we know this, we can make suggestions that appeal to their goals, which is to tell the story better. To help a child tell his story better suggest adding more information, by asking questions. In the child's mind, his picture of a picnic in the mountains contains all the necessary information. Me, Dad, Mom, a zigzag line suggesting the mountain range. It is complete and he may say, "I'm done." Assist in helping the child recall more details. Ask questions that may inspire him to add more to the picture. What kind of food did you eat? Did Dad wear his cap? What did we eat on: a blanket, a picnic table? What else did you see in the mountains? Did you see trees, flowers, rocks, or a stream? All of these things can be suggested in an easy conversation and the child will get more ideas for his or her work. Dr. Charles Gaitskell, author of *Children and Their Art* stated, "Since art is highly personal in nature, the creating person must be the controlling agent of the activities which engage him. To be in control of his work the artist must enjoy a high degree of freedom in the choice of both subject matter and manner of expression." If a child does not want to add more, do not force it, realizing that he may be getting tired of the process or he may not see the suggestion as important to telling the story that he set out to tell. If a child does not want to create at any time, she will need help from you to get her going. Suggest she draw the things she loves. All children have interests. Use those interests to engage her in art-making. Once an attempt has been made, sincerely encourage by pointing out the things you like about the picture. Display the picture to let her know it is important to you. Children who make art have parents who appreciate it!

When you realize in your daily activities that you and your child are having an experience that has the potential of becoming art, ask awareness questions. Helping your child notice the details will give him more to think about later on when drawing.

Picture Talk

Claude Monet. *Jean Monet on his Horse Tricycle*, 1872. Photo Credit: Dover Publications Inc., NY.

Here the artist paints his son, Jean, on his horse tricycle. It is one of Jean's favorite activities. What other things did the artist put in the picture? Does Jean wear a hat? How many wheels does the tricycle have? Can you find the rose bush? Does Jean ride on a path? The artist has added many things to the picture to tell us more about Jean and his horse tricycle.

Favorite Things Project

Use markers to draw a picture of your favorite things. Today you will go to your bedroom or playroom, where you keep most of your favorite things. Walk around the room with your mommy and find something you like. Tell her why it is your "favorite" or "best" thing. Do you like the color, how it feels, or what it does? Do you like it best for daytime play or at night when you go to sleep?

Allowing your child to verbalize her thoughts and opinions helps her gain confidence in her decision making. If your child is having trouble with this activity, you go first and talk about your favorite things. Part of making a child more aware involves showing and sharing who you are with your child. These types of conversations build communication skills as children organize their thoughts in order to give reasons for their preferences.

Hold markers like this. Don't press hard.

Watermelon is Ariel's favorite food so she drew the watermelon below. She saw the outside edge and drew that in black. Then she saw the dark and light green stripes on the side. She drew back and forth to color the stripes.

If your child does not willingly fill in spaces after being shown that she can, let some time go by before reintroducing the idea.

Always remember to put the cap back on the marker after you are finished using it! This will keep your marker moist.

Grown-up Talk
Inventing a Story

Even very young children can make up a story. Pretend play is all about this. When children pretend with pencil and paper, it is play or entertainment. If we keep in mind that children are playing, pretending, making things up, then we realize that this type of art is definitely not about the final product. It is ALL about the process. This is the first lesson I learned about children and their art. My son was four and drawing a wonderful picture of two ships. He put little men all over the ships along with flags and sails. I looked over his shoulder and thought, "This is a keeper." I came back later and was horrified that he had scribbled all over the paper. However, as I looked more carefully at what he was doing, I noticed that he was playing on the paper just as he would with his little Lego pirate figurines. The scribbles were lines of action following balls fired from cannons, the swish of sword blades, and the splash of things hitting

the water. The final picture is shown here, with much of the detail covered up. I have since seen many children, young boys especially, play on paper. I've also noted how their art work develops in the future and noticed a highly developed sense of space. As he got older, my son was able to visualize and draw dinosaurs twisting and turning in ways that were quite inventive and accurate. Most children draw objects like that from a side view with no twisting of the neck or tail. Visualizing a scene on paper may take odd-looking forms when children are young and will not look like typical drawing formulas, but allow it to happen and just watch where it takes them. Children are always learning. When a child draws a story on paper, he is imagining and developing a complicated narrative. He is drawing at the same time the story in being created in his mind. He can see it, change it, and can eventually tell you about it. This kind of mental activity is practice in creative thinking, planning, and foresight that will be a very valuable tool in learning all kinds of subjects.

Create an environment that encourages thinking and drawing. Eliminate noise and distractions, especially visual ones, from sources such as the television and computer. Audio sources are not usually distracting for children. Make drawing tools accessible at all times, even if that is simply pencils and paper. Choose the materials you feel your children can handle responsibly. Paints and messy materials can be stored high and brought out at special times when you are present.

Picture Talk

Mabel Lucie Attwell. Photo Credit: Dover Publications Inc., NY.

Sailors went on journeys far out into the ocean. The water and light played tricks on them and many thought the fish and sea creatures looked part human. They came back telling stories of mermaids, which were half fish and half human. Artists drew pictures of what they imagined mermaids looked like. These boys are fishing with a net. Do you think the mermaid might be hiding? What does she hide behind?

Telling a Story Project

Read "Harold and the Purple Crayon" by Crockett Johnson to your child. I especially love how Harold "drew up the covers" in the end. This project could be great fun using a roll of paper on a hard floor, giving the child lots of room to travel. It could be revisited many times.

Harold created a story using his purple crayon. He went many places and saw many things. He had to think about those things in his mind before he could draw them and see them. Where could you go with your crayon? Choose a crayon or favorite marker. Go on an adventure like Harold went on. Draw where you will go with your crayon or marker.

Children's story drawings will usually have a high amount of detail. This picture was drawn during a church service. When asked about the story, the child replied that the children are happy because the angels are giving them notes from Jesus to say that He loves them. When questioned about the drawings under the ground, she said that the mice families were getting letters too, so they were happy. It's quite a lovely story and one that would have never been told, had I not been curious enough to ask. Ask your children to tell you about their pictures. They will love sharing what they have created with you. Don't say, "What is it?" Say, "Wow, I like this. Tell me about it."

Angels Delivering Letters, by Laurel, age 5.

Grown-up Talk
Beyond Seeing

Adults tend to accept the idea that making art is all about seeing, and have the idea that the more realistic something looks the better it is. Children do not separate their senses into categories as adults do, resulting in a deeper more spontaneous depiction of their experiences even though the art may be hard to decipher. A child may draw what something looks like, feels like, sounds like, or acts like. They will use lines to show how something feels to them or how something moved from one place to another on the page. They will use colors that have more to do with their ideas about that color than the color of the object. Don't expect drawings to look realistic at this stage of development. Realistic drawing will happen naturally when the child is developmentally ready and given opportunity to observe their world.

Both of these pictures show a child's perception of touch or what something feels like. The wolf on the left is primarily fur, with little outline. The picture of Mommy on the couch was drawn from direct observation as the child drew from the floor. When asked what the scribbles were on the bottom of the picture, the child replied that it was the carpet. The feel of the carpet was a large part of her experience as she observed her mother.

When purchasing crayons or markers, give young children many color choices. Young children will use color "as is" without layering or mixing. They enjoy finding the "right" color from among many color choices.

Picture Talk

Claude Monet. *The Artist's Son Asleep*, 1867-68. Photo Credit: Dover Publications Inc., NY.

In this painting, a baby sleeps. Everything around the baby looks soft. The pillow is soft. The child's clothing is soft. Can you find the doll? How do you think the doll feels? Is the baby in a crib with cushioned sides?

Me Project

You wear clothes that are made from fabric. Fabrics can be soft or rough, or bumpy or smooth. Your clothes might also have buttons or a zipper. Your hair might feel curly and tight, bumpy if braided, spiky or smoothly combed. Touch what you have on and touch your hair now. How do they feel? Draw a picture of you. Make it big so that you can add fabric for clothes. Glue on fabrics, yarn, or other materials that Mommy provides for you. Dress yourself up!

Laurel drew a picture of herself on a large piece of paper. She included her belly button. Then she glued squares of fabric that Mommy cut for her onto the picture to make a dress, covering up her belly button. She added yarn for hair on her head. Laurel is happy (smiling with teeth) and likes this picture very much!

Grown-up Talk
Inventing a Language of Symbols

One challenge children will face as they continue to make art is how to communicate their ideas through pictures. We communicate to others on so many levels: verbally, through the written word, through our facial expressions, and our actions. Art is another available source of communication. It may even be a necessary one when cultures mix and language barriers stand in the way of clear communication. In a foreign land, kindness is expressed by a smile, but when one needs to find the local airport, a quick drawing of an airplane may be the best way to communicate the idea. Everyone should have the arts available as another way to communicate ideas. Children are faced with the challenge of communicating an idea as soon as they leave the manipulation stage. They will have to create their own symbols or rely on the symbols they see others have already created. This stage in the child's growth presents one of the biggest challenges to the parent. Some feel inadequate to teach art because they have not developed a language of symbols that they use themselves, while others readily show their child quick and easy steps to draw a sun, dog, stick figure, etc. Neither approach is the best approach. It is important, for development at later stages, to teach children how to invent their own language of symbols through observation. Any parent can guide their child to see more. Look at real objects. Focus on outside edges. Allow your child to draw these things in the ways that he or she decides. When drawing from observation children are more pleased with their works in the end, because the marks truly are their own inventions!

Many art instruction books don't really teach children the processes we use when we make art. Instead, they are activity books in disguise. Activity books require children to follow directions set up by an adult and students are right or wrong in their choices or judged good or bad according to how much their final product looks like the adult's model. This is not training in creativity, exploration of one's own ideas, decision making, imagination, original thinking, or material handling. It lacks all those things that an art education should give a child and offers only limited experience in cutting, pasting, and drawing a line from here to there. Activity books should be restricted to math, language, and those subjects in which there truly is only one right answer. Activity books that are designed to teach art will not harm creativity if the child is also drawing their own images on empty sheets of paper, which we highly encourage. However, if the child is given only activity books they may learn to rely on the adult models presented and not go through the experimentation needed to develop their own language of symbols. To encourage a child to invent their own way of showing certain objects point them to the objects themselves. Run your pencil point along the outside edge of the object. Ask your child to do the same. This helps him to see the object as a shape. Then ask your child to draw the outside edge on paper.

So what does a symbol look like? A symbol is not a realistic representation, but a series of marks used repeatedly to show a specific object. The beauty of symbols is that the closer an adult is to a child, the more readily the symbols can be read. Teachers very often misread symbols and jump to conclusions about children that are simply not truth. Outsiders often looked at the work of my first two children and read into all the action, monsters, frowning faces, and thought they were troubled. Actually, they were very well adjusted, lived in a home full of joy, and thoroughly enjoyed the adventure stories we read often. They loved to draw the anti-climax of the stories, the part where the bad guy almost wins, because that is the most exciting part. My youngest daughter's first symbols were of snakes. She drew many pictures of them! An outsider could read all sorts of negative attributes attached to this reptile. However, as a parent who knows my child, I know that she and her siblings received large, cuddly, stuffed snakes for Christmas. She wrapped it around herself and fell asleep inside it often, using it as a pillow. To her, a snake was connected to fun play with siblings, and the comfort of dosing off to sleep. Below is a picture of her and some of her drawings from that time.

The flame-like shape extending from Daddy's hand in both of these pictures is his pocket flashlight, which the kids were fascinated by and which he offered to them when needed. Here my oldest daughter draws pictures of herself with a book and one of her learning to ride a bike. The flashlight appears in each, drawn in the same way (a flame-like protrusion extending from his hand). She has developed her own symbolic language for showing the flashlight in pictures involving her and her father.

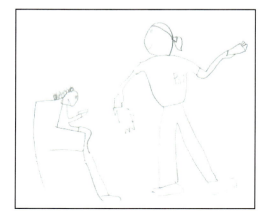

Picture Talk

Claude Monet, Cat Sleeping on a Bed, c. 1865-70. Photo Credit: Dover Publications Inc., NY.

Can you find the sleeping cat in this picture? Where is the cat's head? Where is the cat's tail? Where are the cat's ears? The cat has curled into a ball. The artist drew the cat with colored chalks while it slept. The artist drew the cat the way he saw it.

Direct Observation Project

You can draw pictures of people, animals, and anything else you want to draw by looking at them. When we look at something, the thing tells us where to make the lines. This young girl draws a picture of Daddy. Daddy sits and reads a book so she can see him more easily. You can make a picture while looking at the thing you are drawing. Find an object and draw it using markers, crayons, or other kinds of marking tools.

Artist age 4

Artist age 3

The two pictures above were made at a zoo. The young artist looked at male and female lions.

The figure to the right of the lions was drawn after the artist saw a man blowing a horn at an outdoor concert.

On the right, people have bodies made up of straight lines. How would you draw a body?

Artist age 4

34

Grown-up Talk
Opportunity

 10

One of the greatest things we can do for our children is to allow them to have the opportunity to practice art and to encourage their efforts toward their own goals. We can do that more easily when we see that making art is a "whole mind" activity that benefits them in ways too numerous to count. Dr. Charles Gaitskell writes in his book, *Children and their Art*, "The person engaged in artistic matters harnesses and directs his intellect and emotions, relates himself to his environment, and attempts to bring order out of disorder. The greatest personal disciplines must be exerted if an expressive act is to be successful and worthwhile goals achieved." (9) With so much of the whole person engaged we can understand the necessity of a non-distracting environment. Children rarely create in a room with a TV turned on. Those who know that they will have some free-time every day for pursuing their own creative ideas will produce more that those who do not have this time. One of my children had difficulty with some school subjects. After an exhausting day the habit of sitting in front of the TV during afternoon hours was formed. Realizing that this was ultimately hurting her, I simply did not allow the TV on at all. At first she seemed lost, and then she began to spend quiet time in her room, reading, playing, or listening to stories on tape. Soon the scissors and paper were taken out and within a few months she'd created her own photo album from scratch, a comic book, and a large poster for her room and quite a few drawings of her dog. The free time allowed her to restore her energy and be creative too. The ability to create something from nothing begins in the mind. The mind must be still long enough to rest and to then generate new ideas. As parents we need to trust that free-time and time spent day-dreaming are not wasted time.

> Children need to have opportunity to draw and paint and to invent when they get the urge. Keep a box of odds-and-ends that includes paper tubes, small boxes, buttons, scraps of colored paper, fabric, wrapping paper, ribbons, your scrap booking scraps, and leftovers. It is amazing how children will use raw materials to make something "special". Children at young ages will often use things "as is" so cut fabric into one and two inch squares. Cut paper in 5 inch squares so that it is easy to handle.

Picture Talk

Sharaku, The Actor Morita Kanya, 1794. Photo Credit: Dover Publications Inc., NY.

This Japanese actor is remembered because an artist made a picture of him. Because he is an actor, makeup was placed around his eyes and on his lips to make his facial expressions stand out on stage. His eyebrows are painted as well. What parts of this actor's face are not painted with makeup?

Puppet Project

What can you make from the things you find in an odds-and-ends box? You could make a puppet that opens its mouth as it talks. Start with a small paper bag. Color a mouth on the fold. Color the face. Add extra pieces for hair or ears. Add hands or clothes by cutting out pieces of paper or fabric. Add buttons, ribbons, or whatever you imagine. Once it dries, put the sack over your hand and use your fingers to make the mouth move as you speak for the puppet.

Children love to play. Mix art and play together in this project and your child will get the best of both worlds. There are many craft books in public libraries that will give you more ideas for easy crafts that children can do. Crafts are great for this age when children handle the materials on their own and when the results are praised for themselves, not for how much they look like the example.

Section Two

Use Real World Examples to Point Out Artistic Ideas

As parents apply the ideas found in this section of the book, they will be creating experiences. Before beginning, parents should ask themselves whose experiences they want to see on paper. If it is their own, then they will likely "help" a child by drawing for him and in essence, they will be asking the child to be a mind reader and put on paper what the parent expects to see there. One can see that this is not a fair approach and yet adults often do this to children. Entire curricula are built around the idea of the child following the adult example, proving that this is a mode of thought engrained in the educational system. The focus in this type of thinking is on the end result and being able to "grade" or "evaluate" the educational value of the experience. However, it fails to take into consideration all we learned about the natural development of children and their art as presented in the first section. If it is the child's experience that we want to see on paper, then we will allow free expression while the child is drawing. All the teaching will take place before the marks touch the paper. Parents can do a lot to expand a child's experience by talking about the art and about what they see in the world. Parents can share their experiences verbally and point to what they are talking about so that the child sees a real world example of whatever art concept is being introduced.

One difficulty for most adults is the notion of good or bad craftsmanship by our children. We wonder what others will think of sloppy results and we may not like displaying "messy" pictures. If this is a problem, it helps to realize that in order to learn and gain the skills of cutting, pasting, and mark-making each person must practice those things using their own hands. The more we practice the more skills are gained. Art instruction that is colored or partly drawn in and simply asks the child to cut out, paste on, or finish, is not an art lesson. These types of activities should remain in workbooks about specific subjects, where the goal is to help the child to remember a story or facts, by reinforcing it with pictures. If art education is the goal then the result should be to make an original work of art. A child must work with the tools in order to gain the experience needed to progress. As parents and teachers, we can demonstrate how to use materials one time, then step in again only if a child seems frustrated or is having difficulty. For example, I always step in when a child is holding the scissors upside-down or in an awkward manner, which makes this difficult task nearly impossible and always leads to discouragement. I don't step in when a child is figuring out how to draw what is in front of him, even when he or she has trouble and needs to

try again. It usually works the second time, because he learned something through doing it the first time. While the ultimate goal does include fine craftsmanship, that day is in the future. The goal today is that the child had an experience where skills were practiced. Rewarding art experiences happen only when a child can say, "I did this!"

Become familiar with a child-like approach to drawing and abandon any idea of weighing children down with adult drawing practices. Avoid comments such as, "It should be done like this," "that's the wrong way," or "let me do that for you." Realize that a child's approach will not involve planning, rough sketches, or drafts.

Most children use colors "as is" and do not mix or consider value changes. The act of drawing and choosing colors is a direct response to what they are thinking or seeing so it is all "in their heads." Since we cannot see what another person has envisioned, we are not capable of "helping" when children are creating from their heads. Frustration is often the result for parent and child when the parent tries to step in.

Drawing instruction is not really learning how to draw, but involves learning how to see. We do want to give children examples of how to use the materials and good drawing techniques, but realize that the ideas that we expect to see in adult or grade school work are not the first step, nor are they useful to children at the ages of 3, 4, 5, or even a few years older. What we can teach children within this age group is how to see. It is a focus that they can keep for their whole lives and they will build on it by seeing more and more. The next section will present ideas on how to teach children to see by using real world examples. We will focus on the world they love and the world they care about. Children draw pictures of themselves, their dog, daddy, and the tree in their back yard. We teach art using the very familiar world that exists in their experiences.

Realistic rendering and compositional ideas are learned but creativity, vision, and self-expression are inborn and simply need to be allowed. At all ages, allow children to be creative by encouraging and appreciating their art. At the right time, when they are ready for it, usually around fourth grade, we can teach the technical aspects of art.

Grown-up Talk
Creativity

A creative thinker will push past the boundaries of a given assignment and often fail during those first attempts. A successful result may require more materials and more attempts, but the learning that takes place in the process will far outweigh the expense. Encourage children to be solution finders rather than rote followers when it comes to the arts. Adults can best encourage creativity by asking a child to make limited choices whenever appropriate. Questions such as, "Which color of apples shall we buy today?" as you stand in front of the apple display or "Would you like to wear your blue or your purple socks with that skirt?" while holding each up for the child to see, allow the child to think about his preferences. When allowed to make a few choices a child becomes confident that when given choices, his choices are respected and acted on. This child will have no difficulty making decisions concerning his art. Parents who understand and encourage the artistic process of decision making, trial and error, and experimentation are helping children learn about the processes needed to effectively use art materials.

These are examples of how children experiment with mark-making in order to create a language of symbols: marks that stand for the objects they wish to represent.

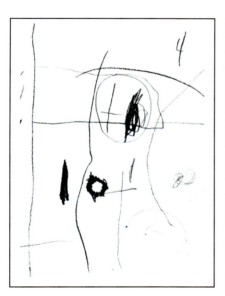
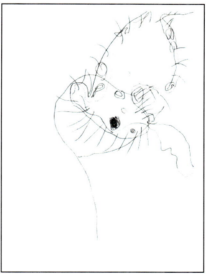
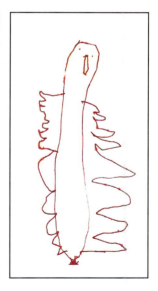

Three, four, or five year olds may not use the whole sheet of paper and may go through many sheets while working out their ideas. Rather than limiting paper use and thereby inhibiting their output, purchase cheap paper. Reams of copy paper, purchased in office supply stores can be found in sizes from 8 ½" x 11" up to 11"x17". Look for markdowns on already cheap products like crayons, markers, and watercolor paint during back-to-school sales in July and August. Do not purchase inferior products to save a few pennies. See page four for some recommended products.

Picture Talk

Georgia O'Keeffe, *Evening Star III*. 1917. Photo Credit: Dover Publications Inc., NY.

In this painting, the artist starts at the center with a yellow ball, which we know is a star. What color is painted around it? What color follows that color? Do the lines seem to follow each line before it? What color are the lines near the bottom of the painting. The artist calls this painting the evening star. How do you think this image is like an evening?

My Hand Project

When artists draw a picture, they look at the outside edge of the things they draw. The outside edge is called an outline. Find the outside edge of your hand and make a picture of it. Pick up a crayon in your favorite color. Place the other hand in the center of your paper. Draw a LINE around the outside edge of the hand that is on the paper. You just made a picture of your hand by drawing around the outside of it! Add some more lines to make the picture interesting. Draw a LINE around the first outline. Follow that by another and then another until the lines go all the way to the edge of the paper. Use as many colors as you like.

In this project children learn that in order to make a recognizable object, they should look at the outside edge of the object. This is a first step from scribbles toward representational drawing. Even if your child is already drawing objects, it is a very fun project! Children can draw a different type of subject (foot, shell, toy, etc.) and proceed with lines around the first outline. This type of activity builds confidence for the beginner.

Grown-up Talk
Invite the Story

Children have a deep desire to communicate with the adults in their lives about their own unique experiences. Art is one of the easiest types of communication children have available to them. Those first efforts to put marks on paper to tell a story or represent an object are absolutely precious. Every child is unique and has something important to say. My most thrilling moments as a teacher are when children tell me about their drawing or painting and I see that what may have looked like scribbles or unconnected blotches of color is really a very direct communication of the unique and worthwhile thoughts and experiences of another individual.

Invite openness. Invite conversation. Never look at the work of a child and say, "What is it?" In doing so the child is told that he or she does not draw well enough for us to see what it is. Instead, point out something wonderful in the work. "Oh, look at those bold swirling lines!" or you might say, "I really like the way you used red all over your painting. It's a beautiful color." Follow the sincere compliment with, **"Tell me about your picture."** Children are quite ready to tell someone who admires their work ALL about it. Be ready to listen to the whole story. By doing so, information is gathered and you can now talk about the specifics of their work with them.

Painting requires water for rinsing the color out of the brush. Fill an empty tuna can with water until about ¾ full. The wide, flat base of the can will not be easily tipped over. There will be fewer spills.

Poster paint can be purchased in liquid form or dry powder form. Use powder only if you enjoy mixing a new batch up each time your child paints. For fewer spills, pour each color in a small jar and place the jars in an open box. Very young children have trouble remembering to rinse the brush between colors. Place a brush in each color so that they can just grab the color needed and return it to the same jar. Use jars with lids, such as baby food jars, so that you can store the paint for the next use.

Picture Talk

Edgar Degas, The Mante Family, c. 1884. Photo Credit: Dover Publications Inc., NY.

This painting shows us a family accompanying a young girl to her ballet class. Art helps us tell others about what we have done. Have you gone to a class to learn something new? What kind of class did you go to?

What I Did Project

When learning involves physical movement, children more easily commit the experience to memory, making it a great activity to draw later. Give your child a hands-on experience with you. You could…
- Make a batch of cookies, allowing the child to handle ingredients, cups, and mixing spoons, while feeling the difference between flour, sugar, and salt.
- Take a trip to a park to look for things to touch. Talk about how different objects like bark, grass, stones, cement, and plants feel.
- If your talents are in music or dance, have children play musical instruments or just beat on a pan to the rhythm of music played on CD. Join in. Then dance around the room to some music while being butterflies, horses, and other animals the children think of.

Do you remember what you did with Mommy (Daddy)? Can you draw a picture about what you did? The picture can include the people who were there. Did a brother or sister join in the fun? The picture can include the objects you saw and touched. Can you draw those things in your picture? The picture can show what was around you. How can you show (the kitchen, the sky, the room you danced in)?

Hold a brush like this.

This child's work shows a family walking with their dog. The family passed a brick firehouse. Figures and dog are in black.

Grown-up Talk
Visual Awareness

Artistic ideas can be explored in ways that work with the natural curiosity children have about their world. When children are young, it is important to help them become more visually aware of their surroundings. People often assume that the first step to teaching art has something to do with demonstration in using paper and pencil and forget that information has to come in before we can expect it to be expressed outwardly in the form of a picture. Teaching a child to become visually aware of their surroundings is always the first step and some parents do this naturally, almost accidentally, by pointing out beautiful sunsets, the variety in a bed of flowers, or taking trips to the zoo to observe the animals at the child's pace. Any parent can do this type of purposeful exploration of the natural world very easily and invite their children to "look" and enjoy the moment. Occasionally you may want to help a child connect what they see to the concept of showing that object in pictures. While viewing the flower group above, the question could be asked, "What color would you pick to show this bright flower?" This type of question is tied directly to something you are both observing. It is not the same as criticizing a child for coloring a tree pink instead of green. When working out of his head, a child should be able to choose any color, because some trees in bloom are pink or he may just feel like using that color at the moment.

Crayon boxes are difficult for little ones to use when it is time to pick up. For storage, put crayons into a flat container with a lid. Some children prefer to separate blues, reds and pinks, yellows and oranges, and dark colors into different containers, making it easy to compare color groups. Tin cans work well for this. Label the containers with construction paper of the same color. This makes pick-up time fun!

Picture Talk

Claude Monet, The Artist's Garden at Vetheuil, 1880. Photo Credit: Dover Publications Inc., NY.

Three figures walk in the garden. Can you find them? The garden is filled with sunflowers. Do the yellow petals remind you of the sun?

Plant Project

Visit a botanical garden, your own garden, a neighbor's garden, or the garden department of your local hardware store. Talk about the plants you see. Draw on the spot or when you get home. Here are some things to look for.

- Petals and leaves have different shapes. What are some of the shapes you see?

- Some flowers have many petals and some have only a few. Which flowers have many petals? Which have only a few petals? How many petals does this flower have?

- Flowers come in different colors. What colors do you like best? What colors look good when sitting near each other?

- If you could choose a flower to plant in a garden of your own, which one would you choose?

Draw a plant that you like best. What does the stem look like? Is there more than one? What shape are the leaves? Does the plant have petals? What color are the petals? What color are the leaves? You can add color to your drawing using paint.

Grown-up Talk
Absorbing Pictures

14

If we think about how children learn to speak, to walk, or to act socially, we know that knowledge is somehow absorbed from real interaction with speaking, walking, and socially engaged adults. We do not get out a teaching manual to teach children these things and we do not purchase activity books so they can practice the skills of walking. In the same way, art is not first learned through manuals or activity books, but by looking at paintings and works by the masters. People often assume that if we show real works of art to children that we are expecting them to copy it. We are not asking a child to copy in the sense of making an exact image, but we do expect them to pick up on the ideas of art and then to be motivated to try their own hand at putting marks on paper in whatever manner they are capable of. Children can gain knowledge of art just by looking at worthy images, just as they learn from adults who walk and talk in an adult way. We don't break down our speech for them or get on our hands and knees to demonstrate how they get from a crawl to a walk. We lift them up on their legs, hold them steady and then let them try on their own. If we keep this in mind as we think about teaching art, we clearly see that by showing children beautiful works of art, we are giving them an example of what can be created by the hand of man. This is in addition to nature viewing, in which they are observing those things created by the hand of God. Charlotte M. Mason, considered by many to be the founder of the Home Schooling movement, states the following.

> "We recognize that the power of appreciating art and of producing to some extent an interpretation of what one sees is as universal as intelligence, imagination, nay, speech, the power of producing words. But there must be knowledge and, in the first place, not the technical knowledge of how to produce, but some reverent knowledge of what has been produced; that is, children should learn pictures…by reading…pictures themselves. Children learn, not merely to see a picture but *to look at it*, taking in every detail."

Where can we find these worthy pictures? In Ms. Mason's day, fine art prints were available. Today many books are produced for children showing museum collections. We should not overlook picture books. The second half of the last century brought full color illustration to this industry and artists jumped at the opportunity to make beautiful picture books. Denise Fleming's handmade paper

illustrations for *In the Tall, Tall Grass* will inspire any child. Pencil drawings by Robert McCloskey in *Make Way for Ducklings* and the ink line work of Dr. Seuss are artistic treasures.

How can we make these pictures available to our children? Read books to children, but to do so in a way that will allow them time to absorb the pictures. I have always been as interested in the pictures as the story itself so it came very natural to me to read the words slowly, with expression and enthusiasm, and then to pause a while to absorb the picture before turning to the next page. I have witnessed more than a few times, people reading to their children in a rushed manner, as if getting through that book and onto the next was the primary goal. Absorbing pictures takes time. Enjoy the moment. Enjoy the feel of your child curled up next to you because your child is gaining comfort, enjoyment, and knowledge of language, sounds, and pictures. This is teaching at its best!

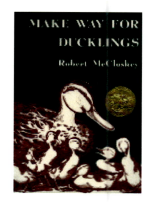

Shortcuts do not teach children how to learn or how to observe. Like sugar for the diet, they appeal to the sense of taste but add nothing to one's healthy development. The following art-related activities should be served in small quantities, if served at all.

Coloring books – these books allow children to make color choices (good) but at the same time limit them to the ideas of others. Consider this a fun time-filler, but not contributing to a child's creative development.

Activity books – these books limit a child's options into two categories: right or wrong. Most decisions that a person makes in their lifetime have many options. A child will learn much more about concepts like up/down, right/left, top/bottom, in/out when given wooden blocks or cardboard boxes and time spent building and constructing. He will also learn about balance and weight, something words on paper can't teach him.

"How to Draw" books – teach tricks that allow children to copy an exact image worked out by someone else, but do not teach how to use the type of tricks that will help them to draw anything that they might want to draw in the future. It trains copyists and there is not a lot of need for copyists in our world today with copy machines and computer printers readily available. These books can be used when a child is having fun with them, but should not be the only art-related activity the child practices.

Picture Talk

Edward Hicks. *Noah's Ark*, 1846. Photo Credit: Dover Publications Inc., NY.

Imagine a story that included every kind of animal on the earth, a boat bigger than anyone had ever seen before, and a huge rainstorm. It is the story of Noah and the ark he built with his three sons. This story has been a favorite subject for artists to paint. It is told in many different ways around the world. Can you find the horses in this painting? Can you find the lion? How many other animals can you name?

Story Book Picture Project

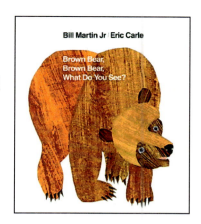

Take a trip to the library and look in the picture book section. Choose many books that have nicely rendered artwork. Read a picture book to your child. Have your child draw a picture of his own, perhaps of a character or image in the book. A good place to start is by reading "Brown Bear, Brown Bear, What Do You See?" by Bill Martin. Animals are shown as large, cut out shapes and the book causes children to think about the colors of animals.

Draw an animal, fish, or bird on a colored sheet of paper. What color is the animal? Can you find paper in that color? Cut out the animal. Where does the animal live? Is green there (Jungle)? Or white (Arctic)? Choose a color that your animal lives in. Glue the cut out animal onto the colored paper you have chosen.

Cutting shapes may be too difficult for a beginner. See page seventy-two for instructions on holding the scissors correctly and beginning skills activities. See page eighty for ideas on using adhesives.

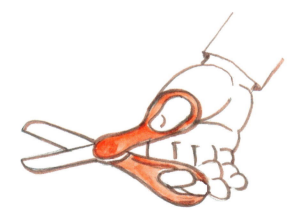

Grown-up Talk
Art to Retell an Event

15

One of the first uses children have for making art is to retell an event. Children remember something that has happened or that happens often and is meaningful to them. These events are filled with details in the child's mind because they were actively engaged in whatever was happening. A child may draw a bear after a visit to the zoo. Titles for their work such as "Me and my brothers playing football," "Me Making Cookies at Grandma's House," and "Snowman in my Yard" tell us the purpose was to put onto paper something from the child's real life experience. One way to engage them in this process is to plan an activity that will give them lots of visual information to use afterward in an art assignment. This is a great opportunity to share your love of something with your child. The more enthusiasm you have, the more engaged your child will be. It could be as simple as making a pie together, or as adventurous as taking a canoe out onto the lake. The more the activity involves the people the child loves and activities those people love, the better the experience. Do be aware that the activity itself may exhaust the child and the art can happen after a good nap or the next day.

This work includes everything needed to effectively tell the story: canoe, the water, sunshine, and me.

Young children use large muscle groups (arms) before using small muscle groups (fingers). Because they first draw with their whole arm, providing them with large sheets of paper may be more appropriate than small sheets. Offer large sheets by purchasing brown or white shipping paper, tearing off large sheets, and see if the response is positive. If your child enjoyed the experience more than when using small sheets, just adjust paper size for a time and then reintroduce small sheets at a later.

Picture Talk

Mary Cassatt, *Children at the Seashore;* 1885. Photo Credit: Dover Publications Inc., NY.

These children have taken a trip to the seashore. They dig in the sand. What do you think they might do next? Will they look for seashells? Will they dip their feet in the water? Perhaps they will enjoy a picnic with their parents.

Trip Project

Where are some of the places you go? What do you see there? Draw or paint a picture of what you see on a trip you have taken.

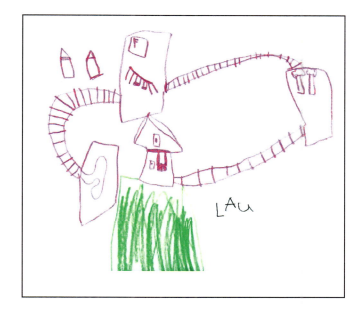

All the student works were drawn after walks were taken through neighborhoods. The one on the top right appears to be a map of the area, while the picture below it shows a girl and her bike. The work on the left shows a young boy and his dog in the middle of a grassy field and near a pond (the blue circle).

Grown-up Talk
The Study

Art helps children become more involved in the world they live in. In our fast-paced media-driven world, we learn to tune out information. Because we can't absorb all the information, we see as we drive through our city streets or watch children's television, our minds learn to edit, to ignore, and to close down what comes in. Art offers balance. Children look carefully at a still object and absorb the intricate details. It's a beautiful activity, really. Children can make art to understand the form of a subject. This type of art does not need a background or to be complete. It is what grown-up artists call a "study". Pick any topic and then go look for it. We did this often in my family. We took walks around the block to look for different shaped leaves. The children found round leaves, pointy leaves, leaves with rough edges, leaves as big as their little sister's tummy, and tiny ones the size of their finger tips. We went to a park to find different kinds of trees. The children found twisted shapes with thick bark, tall thin shapes with smooth bark and a favorite that always remained "our tree". We explored the trees using all of our senses including touching it. We went to the zoo to look at the different kinds of markings on the animal's fur. The children spotted thin stripes, small spots, large loops, wrinkles, animals that were half one color and half another, and more. After exploration exercises like these, have the child draw some of the things they saw. Encourage them with questions. What did the big leaf look like? Did the wrinkly animal have big tusks? Where were the tusks? Encourage the child to "draw the answers" or to "put it on the paper."

Two studies of a real pheasant show how very different children's art can be!

Short sleeves and an apron help keep children clean while making art. Baths afterward are a good solution too!

Picture Talk

Leonardo da Vinci, *Study for the Lost Painting "Leda"*; 1508 and *Branch of Blackberry*; 1504-08. Photo Credit: Dover Publications Inc., NY

This artist drew sketches in notebooks of the things he saw in nature. Above is a study of an oak tree with acorns. Below it is a section of a blackberry bush.

Visual Note Taking Project

Our world is filled with wonderful things that God designed and placed here. Now they grow, live, and move around the earth and we can go out and see those wonderful things. Look for plants or trees. Look for the animals or insects that use those plants in some way. Take notes about the plants and animals you see. You do not need to use words.

You can paint or draw a tree. You can make notes about the kinds of bark or leaves that you find by placing a paper over the bark or over the leaf and rubbing a crayon over it. Display all your notes on trees together on a colorful background.

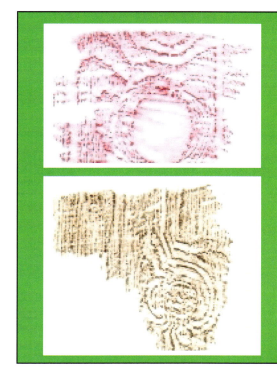

59

Grown-up Talk
Encouragement

Encouragement can come in the form of nice words, but there is more to it than that. One of the most encouraging things we can do for children when it comes to art is to let them know and feel that they can make mistakes without criticism. Allowing for mistakes, do-overs, and lots of tries means that you will not hesitate to offer another sheet of paper to the one who just feels he needs to start over. Perfectionism fights against experimentation, a very necessary component of creativity. When the focus is on the results and not enough on the enjoyment that comes from the process, children become dissatisfied and unable to try new ideas for fear of failure. Never redo or touch up a child's work. This sends a message to the child that it was not good enough. One young boy that I met had this problem. He feared that what he could do was not good enough. He joined my class at 5 years old with his twin. "I can't draw," he said to me. My encouragements were turned negative in his mind and his energies which were not poured into the

creative process showed up in acting out against other students. He would look over their shoulders and say, "That's no good." I pulled him aside to lay a few ground rules for the class. No criticizing. Back at his table, he looked at his brother's work. "Is that any good?" he asked me directly and sincerely. "Yes, it is," I replied, "your brother is looking at what is in front of him and drawing what he sees." "Oh," he said simply, and he jumped into the process of putting his own marks on paper for the first time. The focus for him was now on the process, not on the results. From this point on, he made art freely.

Teaching a child to hold a crayon, pencil, or other marking tool correctly will ensure that you will not have to re-train later when the child begins to write. As the child gains more and more control of the tool, and makes marks go where he wants them to, he will find much satisfaction in the process. This project is great fun and can be accomplished successfully even if a child is not yet drawing objects.

Picture Talk

Berthe Morisot, *The Cradle*; 1872. Photo Credit: Dover Publications Inc.

We all start out very small and then grow bigger. In this painting by Berthe Morisot, a mother looks at her small child. The child is lying in a beautiful cradle. Fabrics hang from above. Look at the mother's face. What do you think she might be thinking? What is the baby doing in the picture? Do babies sleep a lot? Do babies eat? Do babies play? You do many more things than a baby does now that you are bigger. In this next project, you can make art that shows people how big you are!

How Big I Am Project

A picture is made to show others something you know or see. What can you tell people about you? Use a picture to tell others about you. Start with a large roll of paper. Tape the paper down on a hard surface, like the floor. Lie on the paper and hold still while Mommy draws a line around your whole body. When she has finished, you color in everything that is you. Color your eyes, mouth, hair and clothing. You can add toys or things you like in the picture too!

Expect children to draw eyes, ears and other features from angles different from that of the outline. Enjoy the surprise and unexpected results.

Grown-up Talk
Seeing the World Through a Child's Eyes

Three, four, and five year olds and even older children are not aware of the whole space of the page, as a professional artist is. Filling up the whole paper with color can be taught or demonstrated, but do not rush children who are resistant to the idea. It simply does not fit their goals. Children are thinking about the "things" or "objects" within the painting, not the painting as a whole or as an object in itself. Therefore, we often see in their pictures that grass sits along a thin line at the bottom of the page because grass is beneath us. The sky is a thin line of blue across the top because sky is above us. In between the grass and sky is where all the activity takes place, so the figures are placed there, with white space around them. In the scene above the child felt finished once he had completed the outline of the figure and dog, a grass line, black dashes to show the direction that the ball and dog travel, and yellow outline of the clouds. We can see that the figure is throwing a ball for the dog to fetch so every necessary "thing" had been included. When it was suggested that the clouds be surrounded with blue sky, the student willingly added the blue and then proceeded to fill in the green shirt and brown dog. This makes the picture more colorful and interesting and since it was only suggested, this picture remains fully the work of the child's own hands and mind.

Children often use only outlines to show objects. One way to make them more aware of the idea of filling in an outline with color is to have them rub their hand over the surface of objects. For example: An outline of a boat has been drawn and I want my son to fill in the space with color. I can demonstrate that space in the real world by going out with my son and taking our hand across the outside edge of the

boat, I say, "This is what you've drawn. The outline is the outside edge." Now we rub our hands across the side of the boat. "This is the side of the boat. What color is it?" Can you find that color and color in the side of the boat in your picture?" Now the child has a real world experience that directly relates to adding color to the picture.

For those that are eager to teach children something of "real substance", the next project will show how to accomplish it in a way that children may use. Teach it in a way that lets the child decide what he will do with the information. Children are amazingly responsive to new information when presented in the right way, a way that incorporates how children think about the world. Here we will use the idea of a horizon line as an example of how to teach complex subjects. A child is not interested in vague concepts like perspective or horizon lines as they are demonstrated in drawing instruction books. He is interested in the "things" or "objects" within his painting. Once the horizon line becomes a "thing" that is noticed, he just may decide to include it in his work. Introduce children to art related topics using real world examples. If you cannot **see** a horizon line, choose another topic that can be pointed out. You could teach on proportion, shapes, filling in spaces, edges or any other element related to an art education, by using real world examples.

For those that feel a child is ready to learn more but have no idea of what that more may be or how to present it, Artistic Pursuits Inc. offers complete instruction in the K-3 Series for five to nine year olds which is easy to use, takes students smoothly through the symbolism stage, and prepares them for the following stage of development: realistic drawing.

Children learn through play. Play can be adult-directed or child-directed. Play is simply free exploration of an interest or objective that involves some mimicking of adult behavior. Allow children to mimic the proper ways to handle materials as you direct that part of the learning. Offer new experiences. Help children become more aware of what they see. Once you have directed the activities in these ways, allow child-directed play to begin. A child can explore how they choose to draw a dog, how they place objects on the paper, when they begin to put more detail into the picture, and all decisions related to the picture itself. When information is offered in the form of showing the idea in the real world and a suggestion, the child will be able to pick it up when he needs it and when he is ready to use it. In this way, we are not pushing children to make adult type images before they are ready to handle that information.

Picture Talk

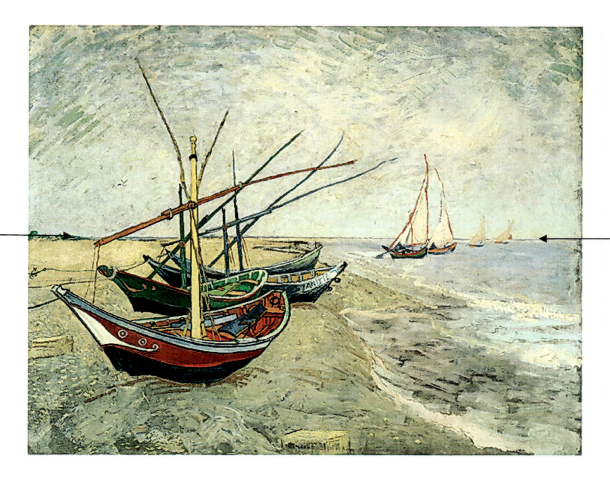

Vincent Van Gogh, *Boats on the Beach at Saintes-Maries*; 1888. Photo Credit: Dover Publications Inc., NY.

What is above you? Is it the sky? What is below you? Is it the ground? Do you know that we can see the place where the sky meets the ground? Sometimes the sky meets the water. Can you find that place in this picture of boats? It is far away. The arrows point to it. We call this edge the horizon.

Horizon Line Project

Some horizons are flat like a straight line. Some horizons curve up and then down a bit, and some are jagged, bumpy edges. If you draw a line in the air across the place where you see the sky meets the ground, what kind of line is it? Draw that line in the air and see.

Some horizon lines are hard to see because "things" are in the way, but the horizon is still there. Can you see the horizon line in this picture? The horizon line is very bumpy because he has drawn a mountain range. Use colored markers, pencils, or crayons to draw a picture from your memory or your imagination. In your picture, show where the sky meets the ground.

This incredible work of art was created by a young student who had never been taught about putting horizon lines on paper, how to overlap objects, or how objects in the distance look smaller and are arranged further up on the paper. Those are the issues for elementary students. However, through observation of the world, he understood those things and put them down on the paper in this beautiful drawing. Children are capable of so much when we encourage them to look at the world they live in!

Grown-up Talk
Where Do They Go From Here?

When we have directed children to become observers of nature and when we have filled their minds with wonderful adventurous stories, the subject of art becomes merely a tool for allowing children to express their own ideas to us about what they have taken in. The amount of teaching is minimal because the adult has simply learned to help children to "say what they want to say, in the terms in which they want to say it" (Gaitskell 43). The challenge for adults is to be aware of the maturing young artist's needs and to meet those needs with proper media, tools, methods, and techniques, while continuing to allow the art produced to remain an expression of the child's experience. This can seem a bit daunting for a parent who has little art experience. It was all taken into consideration while writing the Artistic Pursuits Curriculum for K-12 grades. This program is easy to use with little preparation and no prior knowledge of art needed. At ages five or six, a child will want to learn about what it really is to be an artist. You can introduce them to the things artists do, the way artists look at the world, and the many ways art is used throughout cultures and time, which will give children a broader base for understanding art. Children at this age will continue to work within the symbolic stage of development and symbols will become more complex and varied as children find new and better modes of expression. They are geniuses at creating unique devices to show the meanings of what they wish to express. An important figure, like Mom or Dad, may be drawn larger than a tree or house. This is not unusual, as we see this device used in medieval art to show the importance of Christ, or Mary with the infant Christ. In the child's work and the work by the medieval master, emphasis is given to the most important objects within the painting. Perhaps more difficult to understand is the way color is often chosen simply because the child likes it, rather than for its resemblance to reality. Other devices may include works painted from an aerial view in order to show everything a child wants to show within the picture space. People figures may have lines drawn around them to show that they are inside a room. These inventive methods are valid and show us that a child is thinking, envisioning, experimenting, and growing in knowledge of how to use pictorial space.

At age nine or ten, children enter a new stage. It is as if their eyes are suddenly opened and they become aware of forms, shading, and contours. They have entered a more realistic phase. At this time, children often become dissatisfied with their work. They may be fine one day and the next day they may make

exaggerated claims such as, "I just can't draw anything!" It is no time to make jokes in hopes of lightening the burden they feel to make their art better! In this newly entered stage of realism, offer them a set of ideas or techniques for seeing the world. We call these ideas the elements of art. The elements are the knowledge they crave, though they will not know how to express that to you. Expect children in this stage to become more cautious and to evaluate their work with great intensity of feeling. They will usually continue to use strong lines around the edges of the objects they draw. In order to allow their art to remain an honest expression of their own ideas, while offering them information on techniques, we should continue to have them observe from nature, to use the subject matter of their choice, and to choose the way they want to show that subject, (the arrangement). In this way the art continues to be truly their own.

A more mature stage will be entered as children continue to apply the elements of art in varied situations, so that their experiences are broadened and skills are sharpened. In high school, from ages 14 to18, we desire for each child to enter a stage where the art produced is wholly the artists and is identifiable as such. We identify artists by their style. Style cannot be learned, but is an outcome of making one's own choices. Choices include preferences for art materials (watercolor, charcoal, and pencil), how to handle those materials (light wispy strokes, bold and heavy handed), and subject matter (preference for drawing figures, animals, or landscapes), along with compositional preferences (close up views, overlapping, use of perspective). It is important to note that artists who led the way toward Abstraction of the early 20th century were first highly skilled draftsmen who simply chose to simplify art to fit in with new social ideas. This set in motion the flawed idea that we no longer need to train artists in methods of seeing and drawing. When teachers take the approach of giving the child no technical information while asking him to "create something", the results are usually extremely poor. Added to this problem is the fact that many college art courses skip the introduction to the elements of art and principles of design (valuable knowledge) while completely focusing on creativity and pushing for a style that "breaks past the boundaries." That is why a student, while in high school, should become aware of this base of knowledge and acquire skills in realistic drawing before entering a college program. However, that is a long way off for many of those using this book. For now, enjoy the output of your child and encourage artistic endeavors.

If you have more than one child, there will be the temptation to compare what they produce. You should expect their outputs to be extremely different and to develop within different periods. There is no one stage that a child should enter at a specific age. There is no "better" symbol to use for any particular object. Enjoy the diversity within your own family.

Picture Talk

Have you ever met a happy tiger? I have not. However, as we look at this work by the Japanese artist, Hokusai, it is easy to believe that he has seen one. The title for this print is *Old Tiger in the Snow*. We can see that the tiger is old, because his legs and tail are a little bent and have grown crooked with age. Let's see what else we can find out by looking at this picture.

Hokusai, Old Tiger in the Snow, 1849. Photo Credit: Dover Publications Inc., NY.

Is the snow deep? Is the snow still falling? Can you imagine the tiger catching a snowflake with his tongue? Why do you think the tiger is smiling? Are the tiger's claws sharp? How many claws does he have on each paw? Look at the needles on the tree. Do the needles look like tiger claws in some way?

The Way I SEE It Project

Hokusai drew a tiger that was unusual and different from the way most of us see tigers. An artist draws things in the way he sees them. Each person notices different things about the objects they look at. On this page, you will see how many ways a model of a pheasant can be drawn. Each student drew what he or she saw in his or her own ways. Look at how each one is beautiful, colorful, and original.

Art by Kellen

Art by Kari

Art by Lindsey

Art by Kara

Now you draw a picture of an animal, bird, or fish. Draw either from real life or from a picture if you don't have a real animal, bird, or fish to look at. Draw it the way you SEE it!

Section Three

First Skills

Experimentation is a necessary practice when learning to use art tools and materials. A child may enjoy just snipping pieces of paper when first given a scissors. You will want to provide a few instructions in the use of the tools and mediums you place before your child. Giving your child examples and instruction in proper use of materials will help you avoid large puddles of glue on the table and the snipping off of the baby's first lock of hair. Purposeful experimentation will allow your child to gain skills while leaving the creation open to his or her imagination.

Scissors

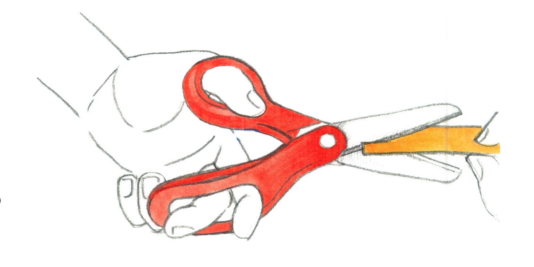

Holding the scissors correctly is necessary for ease of use. Scissors should be held in the hand the child naturally chooses to write with. Hold paper in the other hand, parallel to the table surface. Hold scissors at a right angle to the paper with the thumb in the upper (smaller) hole and the first two fingers (index and middle) in the lower (larger) hole. Good cutting skills are a product of using the tool correctly. Watch your child carefully as he begins. This will ensure that good habits are formed. Children struggle when they use the scissors incorrectly.

Scissors Safety

Provide a good pair of scissors such as Fiskars brand for kids with a blunt end. Young children do not need to use sharp points in their cutting activities. Teach that scissors are an art tool, not a toy. We don't run or play with scissors. We don't' cut our hair or clothing. We only cut art materials like paper and string.

Some bend their wrist back at a sharp angle, holding the scissors upside down even though the hand is correctly positioned in the scissors. Have some fun while correcting children. I say something like, "Oh, you are working very hard by holding the scissors that way. Soon your muscles are going to say, 'Stop! I'm tired!' Hold it this way and make it easier on your muscles so that they can have some fun too."

First Scissor Activities to Strengthen Cutting Skills

Snipping – Prepare 1 inch strips of brightly colored construction paper. Show your child how to hold the scissors and with one cut, snip off a piece from the end of the strip. Let the child snip for any length of time while interest is high. Collect the cuttings. Cut two pieces of wax paper in an identical shape such as a heart, circle, or square. Glue around the edge of one piece. Let your child sprinkle the cuttings inside and then seal with the other wax sheet on top. Place a book on top for weight and allow to dry flat. When the glue has dried, poke a hole through the top of the wax paper shape. Run a ribbon through the hole and tie a knot. Your child has a beautiful art object that contains their special work. You can hang it up on a wall or place on a shelf for display.

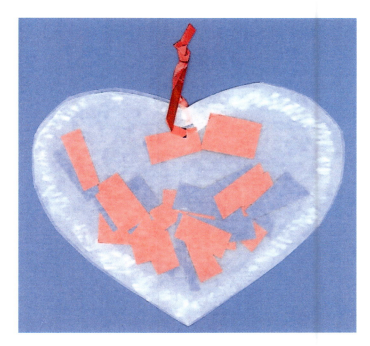

Cutting Paths – Prepare one-inch strips of brightly colored construction paper. Glue or draw an object to a craft stick. Glue or draw a related object at the end of a paper strip. The child is shown how to cut a path so that one object can reach the other. It will look something like this when finished:

Say, "Cut a path through the grass so the squirrel can get to the tree." Once the path is cut, tape the left edge and insert the craft stick through the slit. The child can now move the craft stick back and forth through the cut she made.

Look for pictures in magazines, use stickers, or have your child suggest the subject and draw simple pictures at both ends. This teaches children to control the scissors in order to cut a line without cutting to the edge before they reach the object at the other end. The related objects give a child motivation to concentrate on where the scissors is going. Any failures can be taped and the child can start again so that each strip is met with success.

Expand the idea by drawing curved, jagged, or squiggly lines. When your child has gained the skills, prepare strips in the same manner, but draw the line to be cut. Some ideas are as follows:
A fish swims.
A soldier marches.
A bunny hops.
A frog leaps.

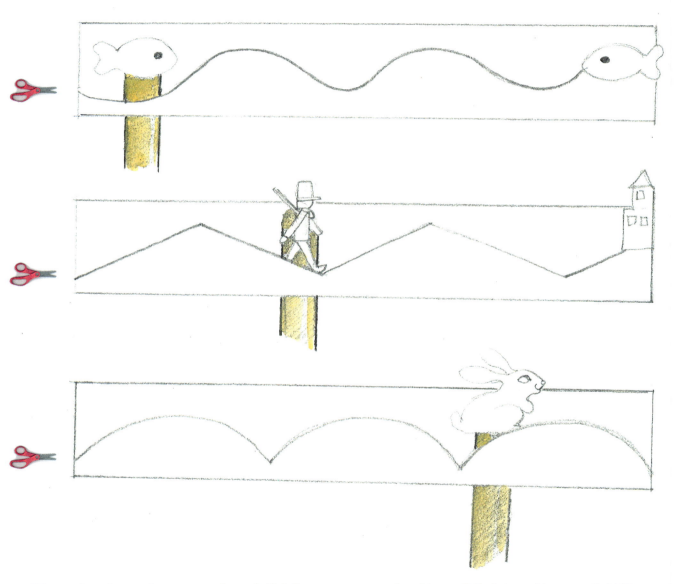

Tape both ends once the child has cut on the line. Making lines of different types is a fun challenge when your child can do it somewhat accurately. Look for ways to introduce the child's favorite topics. Trucks and cars, sea animals, dinosaurs, and anything else can be used. Simple ideas like these can inspire children to work on their own and the longer they practice a skill, the better at it they become.

Cutting Shapes — Cutting a shape is a bit more difficult than cutting lines because the paper must be turned as the child cuts. Cut a half sheet of construction paper so that the piece is easier for little ones to handle. Demonstrate how to draw a large shape on the half sheet. Draw simple shapes such as birds, sheep, etc. Next, let the child cut out the shape by holding the paper in one hand and cutting along the line that was drawn. Do not cut for the child. If the results are a blob, then it is their blob and they can be very proud of creating it from a rectangular sheet of paper!

Give your shapes a home by drawing a large tree for the birds or a green pasture for the sheep. Attach four sheets of construction paper together using glue or tape. Your child can then glue the birds to the tree top or the sheep to the green pasture. A feather or two could be glued to the bird. A few cotton balls could be glued to the sheep if desired.

Allow your child to draw and cut the shapes. It will not look as neat as the examples above, however it will be the child's own creation when completed.

Pencil, Crayon, and Marker

Holding a drawing tool such as a pencil or crayon correctly is necessary for ease of use and future handwriting skills. Have your child open his hand with the forefinger straight, the thumb up, and the other three fingers curved. Lay the pencil into the hand, onto the bending middle finger and between the thumb and forefinger. Have your child grip the pencil with the thumb and forefinger. Complaints about aching muscles indicate that your child is holding the drawing tool too tightly. Tell him to relax. To help him remember, say, "Don't squeeze the pencil tight. Be gentle with it and it will be happy to go where ever you direct it to go." When your child begins handwriting skills, it will be a huge benefit to have developed the correct technique for holding the pencil while drawing.

> Pencil Safety
> Teach children to be still when drawing whether sitting or lying on the floor. Teach them to put the pencil down before moving around. Never run with a pencil in hand. Never poke another person with a pencil. Teach them to use the pencil sharpener when you feel they are ready to do it correctly.

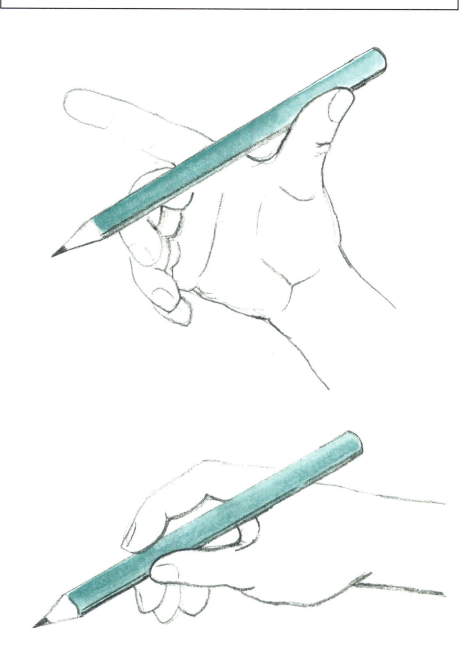

First Pencil, Crayon, or Marker Activities to Strengthen Drawing Skills

Large Motor Skills – While drawing and handwriting both require the use of fine motor skills, drawing has the added benefit of developing the large motor skills as well. These include the movement of the shoulder, the elbow and the wrist as the child learns to draw shapes and lines that extend from one end of the paper to the next. Most children do this quite naturally when first handling drawing materials. However, children who have been trained in handwriting with very little experience in art may not make use of the entire arm, which inhibits their ability to draw large. In exercises such as the following one, using large sheets of paper will help. To demonstrate the movement, draw a large imaginary circle in the air in front of you. Have your child copy the movement. Feel the movement in your shoulder and elbow as you draw the circle. Next, give your child a large pad of paper and pencil or crayons. Markers work well too. Ask her to draw the earth, large and round. Then she should draw hills, trees, houses, and anything else she might see on the earth.

This imaginary drawing requires the use of large muscles as she fills the earth with objects.

Small Motor Skills – To practice small motor skills the child can draw inside a pre-drawn shape. I like to use cookie cutter figures of gingerbread men. Draw around the simple shape. Ask the child to draw the facial features, then to add the extras such as buttons, scarves, hat, and whatever they desire using crayons or colored markers. You can make many of these shapes for them to draw the details into.

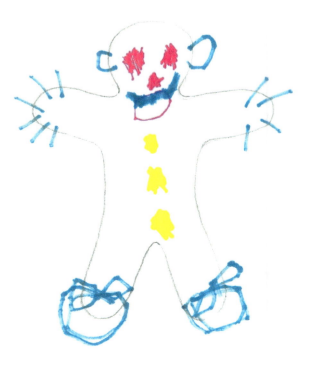

To Rest the Hand on the Paper or Not – Resting the hand on the paper allows the fingers to move out and away from a central point, which can at first help one gain more control of the fine motor skills of writing and drawing details. Unfortunately, it limits the range one can reach, so it is best to rest the hand very lightly. When drawing, the pinky finger may be the only part touching the paper as the artist moves the hand and arm over the surface. Expect young children to rest their hand on the paper and do not worry about smears, which will inevitably happen.

Filling in a Shape – This is how one is usually taught to use crayons and coloring books, but a shape that the child has drawn can be filled in as well. A color is chosen, and then the shape is outlined in that color. This lays down a coating of wax onto the paper and helps one stay within the line. Then demonstrate how to fill in the shape, using fingers to go back and forth while moving the hand just slightly so that the whole space is filled. It takes practice and while it is a worthwhile goal to be able to control the crayon or pencil in such a manner, it is something that is easier to do as the child gets older.

Adhesives

There are many options when it comes to adhesives. The primary goal is to provide a type of adhesive that is easy to use when placed in the hands of very young children and one that will hold the work together so that little hearts are not broken when their masterpieces fall apart. You can use liquid glue, which comes in a bottle, or glue sticks. Hot glue guns and spray glues are NOT recommended for young children and are dangerous to all but adults who can use with the proper precautions. Washable glues come in both liquid and stick forms, but do not hold as well as the more permanent types. Paper can appear stuck and then become un-stuck and the projects fall apart. I use permanent glue sticks, which wash out of clothing and off hands just fine and have better adhesion qualities. Elmer's Glue All has been a favorite for decades but is thinner than it was a few years ago. Kids love the quick and easy use of a quality clear tape such as Scotch Tape. The only reason not to use tape in most projects is that it shows, whereas glue is invisible in the finished product.

First Glue and Tape Activities to Hold Art Together

Glue Stick – Glue sticks are for gluing paper to paper. They are sold in twist or push up tubes. This solid adhesive is convenient but still need s to be handled properly for best use. Young children, fascinated by the twisting will inevitably twist it all the way out of the tube, making messes. Instruct them to twist it only enough so that the glue is above the edge of the plastic tube. Apply it directly to the paper, and then press it down, holding for a few seconds. The problem with glue sticks for young children is that they are not a strong adhesive and they often dry too quickly so that while the object appears to be attached, it comes loose later. When gluing large sheets or areas, teach children to apply the glue around the edges and leave the center.

Children can make a simple picture using snipped pieces of paper and then gluing the back of each snip, one at a time, and applying the snip to a full sheet of construction paper. You can draw a simple outline as in this jack-o-lantern example or cut an object such as a truck from a magazine and have the child use the snipped pieces to create a background.

Liquid Glue using the Q-Tip method – The Q-tip, also called cotton swab, method of using liquid glue works especially well for young children, keeping the glue off hands. Squeeze a pool of white glue, such as Elmer's Glue All, onto a paper plate, bowl, or a small piece of tin foil. Demonstrate to the child how to roll one end of the Q-tip in the glue. Pull it away from the pool of glue and roll it onto a clean part of the plate or bowl to get rid of excess drippy glue.

Drag the Q-tip across the back of the piece to be glued. Flip it over and attach to the paper background.

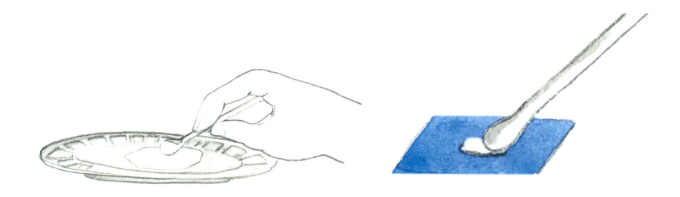

While this method is great anytime you use liquid glue, it works especially well when applying glue to an upright surface such as a can. Help your child with the first part of this project. Wash a can of any size that has been opened at one end. Make sure that there are no sharp edges. Cut a strip of construction paper to fit around the can. Have your child glue the edge of the sheet of construction paper so that when it is wrapped around the can it can be attached. Now your child can cut out pieces from construction paper for eyes, nose, ears, and mouth to make a face on the cylinder. He can use the Q-tip method to dab the glue pieces onto the covered can. The end project can be used as a pencil or crayon holder.

Liquid Glue from the Bottle – When demonstrating how to use a bottle of liquid glue, first adjust the cap so that the glue does not pour out too readily, but does come out easily when the bottle is squeezed. Show young children how to make dots of glue on the back of a piece and then flip and press down. Children like to make dots with the bottle and it is a method that works best. Students should never open the cap all the way and pour a steady stream of glue onto a project. Too much glue causes the paper to wrinkle and creates unnecessary messes.

You may want to try Aleene's Original Tacky Glue, which is thick white glue that stays where it's put. Elmer's also makes tacky glue. This glue can be used to attach things like glitter, feathers, cotton balls, paper, cardboard, wood sticks, cloth, and leather. It dries clear. Remember to keep a good attitude and don't panic when you see your child making a glue puddle. Who isn't fascinated when watching glue as it pours in a stream from the bottle? Liquid glue washes up easily when it is still wet. Use lots of water and everything will come clean.

Glue paper using dots of glue.

Reinforce the idea of using dots by having your child make a dot picture. Using paper punches of different sizes, (these are available at hobby and scrapbooking stores) punch dots of different colors. Show your child how to use a paper punch. Many children love using a tool like this. Then have the child glue the paper dots with a dot or more on the back of each piece and flip and stick onto a sheet of construction paper. If you'd like to make a theme such as bubbles or distant stars in the sky, it will be even more fun.

Tape – Teach a child how to lift the tape, pull out just a small piece, and pull down so that it tears off on the jagged edge of the dispenser. Watch as they use tape and compliment a child for making pieces that are just the right size. It is easiest to use tape on a flat surface and attach one flat piece to another.
Show them how to press the tape to the surface by dragging a finger along it after they have it where they want it. You can make a barn, house, or any type of building with doors that lift up, showing a surprise underneath. Draw the building on a full sheet of construction paper. The child can cut square doors and then tape a top or side edge to the building so that the door can be opened. Tape or glue pictures of what is inside.

Create a loop figure. It could be an animal or bird. Prepare by cutting one inch strips of colored construction paper. Have your child make loops of paper and tape the ends together. Make loops of different sizes for the body, eyes, and other parts. Add different shapes for nose, beak, feet, or paws and have the child secure them with tape. The shapes can be very simple and should be created by the child.

83

Brushes and Paint

Young children love to paint, however one should expect a lot of experimentation and not a lot of control. We do not give specific projects here because most painting techniques are above the abilities of this age group. Techniques can be more limiting to children's imaginations than they are beneficial.

Set up the paints in the following way. Put the paper directly in front of the child on a desk or table surface. Place paint set above the paper or to the side. Do not place paints by the elbow or arm because it is easy for a child to knock them to the floor. Place the brush, water can, and paper towel on the side the child naturally uses to hold the brush; right side for a right-handed child and left side for a left-handed child.

The Brush – Most brushes found in cheap paint sets will be camel hair, as shown on the left. We strongly suggest purchasing a synthetic brush. Synthetic brushes are a reasonably priced alternative for young children and handle much better than camel hair brushes. The bristles are somewhat stiff and do not flatten out or become limp when placed into water. A brush should have this kind of body and should not collapse so that the child is dragging the metal piece, ferrule, against the paper as he paints. Have the child hold the brush in the same way he holds a pencil. Teach the child to drag the brush across the paper and not to hammer with it. It is best to keep the instruction simple.

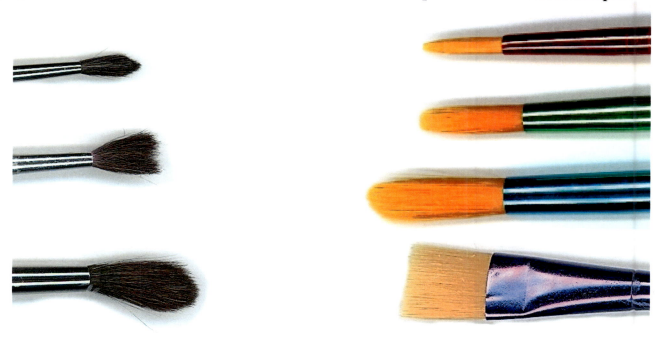

Natural hair brushes, shown on the left, are made from squirrel, goat, ox, pony, or a blend. They are called "pony hair" or "camel hair" brushes, though none are made from camels. They get limp and spread out when wet. Sometimes they are trimmed to a point, as shown on the top, but they lack "snap" and will not return to a point after a brush stroke, making them difficult to control. Natural hair brushes do not maintain their shape as shown in the middle example so children are not able to do detailed work. These brushes do hold a lot of water and are usually sold in watercolor sets. Synthetic brushes, as shown on the right, are made from nylon or polyester filaments. The common name for this type of brush is "Taklon." They are easily maneuverable because the bristles have more strength and come to a point when wet. Round brushes of this type come in different sizes. Flat brushes, shown at the bottom, also come in

different widths. The brushes shown are produced by Crayola®. Another common brush on the market is the bristle brush. It is cheap and made from hog's hair. This very stiff brush spreads thick paints, such as liquid tempera, acrylic, or oil. It does not absorb water well, which leads to messes when using thinner paints.

The Paint – Watercolor paints are dry and are usually found in trays. The lid usually has areas for mixing colors. Provide a can with a wide base for rinse water. To use watercolors, dip the brush in water and then into a paint color. Then apply the loaded brush to paper. Use the water can to clean one color from the brush before beginning to use another color. Extra moisture can be dabbed with a paper towel.

Liquid poster or temper paint is wet and comes in jars. These paints should be poured out onto a sturdy paper plate with edges. I pour quarter size areas of each color onto the same plate. Any paint that says "washable" will be a gel-like substance that does not have as much color saturation as regular paints. The colors will be weak. You may or may not want to use this type of product. Provide a can with a wide base for rinse water. Demonstrate how to rinse the color from the brush before dipping the brush into a different color. This keeps the colors in each space pure. If the preschooler finds it difficult to remember to rinse the brush each time, the colors will become muddy and undesirable to use. The easiest solution to this problem is to pour paints into separate small containers and place a brush in each color container.

Paper - Since children will go through a lot of paper, purchase reams of copy paper from office supply stores or a local department store. Watercolor paper can be purchased as they learn to work longer on each painting. Watercolor paper will hold up better when wet.

The Clothing and Surroundings – Many people dread introducing paint to young children, but children love it. Teach children that the paint is for the paper only. Provide a work area that has surfaces that can be cleaned with water. This includes the wall and floor. Use an old shirt for a paint shirt or get an apron and have them roll up long sleeves. Kitchen tables are usually a great painting area and you can get kitchen work done while keeping an eye on their

progress. Have a plan for moving wet paper to a spot where it can dry. Most children will make more than one picture at a time. In the summer let them paint outdoors!

Working with preschoolers takes patience as they learn to use new materials. It takes understanding when things get messy. It takes faith as you allow the child to do the work and handle the project as best as his skills will allow. It takes a loving parent or teacher who values the child and his or her ability to learn and grow. Thank you for the generous qualities you display as you work with our child. I hope you enjoy making art a part of your child's preschool years. When your child is ready for Kindergarten then he or she is ready for the weekly lessons in *ARTistic Pursuits, Grades K-3 Book One, An Introduction to the Visual Arts,* published by Artistic Pursuits Inc.

Bibliography

Gaitskell, Dr. Charles., *Children and Their Art*, Harcourt, Brace & World, Inc. United States of America, 1958.

Mason, Charlotte M., *A Philosophy of Education*, Vol.6 Tyndale House Publisher, Inc. Wheaton, Illinois, 1989.

Micklethwait, Lucy, *A Child's Book of Art, Great Pictures First Words*, Dorling Kindersley Publishing, Inc. New York, NY